A Wizard in the Kitchen

Magical recipes for kids of all ages

By Abby Hupp
Illustrations by Bill Bronson

A Wizard in The Kitchen

Copyright 2006 by Abby Hupp

Illustrations by Bill Bronson

All rights reserved.

No part of this book may be copied, distributed,

or otherwise reproduced without express

written permission from the publisher.

Published by Plan B Books

www.PlanBBooks.com

ISBN # 0-9785798-0-1

Printed in the USA by

Morris Publishing

P.O. Box 2110

Kearney, NE 68848

This book is for anyone who believes in magic, in all its many forms and in the places it is found.

Very special thanks to the people who helped bring this book to life; My mother and lifelong motivation, Janet Kupferberg; my sister, proofreader and editor Kay Cochran; my very patient and kind attorney Tom Nutter; my dear friend and artist extraordinaire Bill Bronson; and the love of my life, Paul Johnson; for putting up with me during this process.

And of course, the Billington, Kupferberg, Rudolph, Cochran and Johnson families, you are where my heart resides.

Becoming a Wizard in the Kitchen, page 6

Wizarding Levels Explained, page 7

Kitchen Terms and Measurements, page 8

Advice on Safe and Sanitary Cooking, page 10

Foods for Feasting, page 13

Conjuring for a Crowd, page 29

Tricks for Treats, page 44

Powerful Potions, page 61

Becoming a Wizard in the Kitchen

Making delicious food is the next best thing to actually practicing magic. Like the witches and wizards throughout history and our favorite books, you are magically transforming one thing into something different altogether. Certain foods can enchant our senses and invoke feelings of comfort, excitement, awe and more, just like a powerful charm might. Knowing the effects, properties and flavors of herbs, fruits and vegetables is easily compared to the Herb Lore studied by ancient druids. Careful measuring, adding the right ingredient at the correct time and heating it to a specific degree, is exactly what a skilled potion maker does. The healing properties of food needs no further mention than good old chicken noodle soup. It's no wonder that people crave chocolate when they've had a bad day, chocolate has a naturally occurring chemical in it that causes the brain to release a pleasure hormone, making you feel relaxed and happy.

What I consider to be magic can be created out of nearly anything and is indeed found everywhere you look. It cannot be measured; you can't see it, taste it, hold it, smell it or hear it. Or can you? Is there really magic in today's world? The answer is a resounding yes! It comes from deep inside each and every one of us. Once you know what to look for, you will begin to see it everywhere, and be able to tap into your own powers. Cooking is simply the most common method that people can use to perform great feats of magic; using everyday ingredients and one special addition that can't be bottled and isn't sold in stores, *you*. It is the cook that makes the meal magical, not the food. When you are cooking for people you care about, you are actually putting your heart and soul into each dish, making it better than the sum of its parts. This "secret ingredient" can be any combination of passion, love, respect, friendship, compassion, determination and the desire to impress.

Most people have experienced the result of magical cooking in their lifetimes, and my grandmother's chocolate chip cookies are a perfect example. She would mail them to us in a shoebox, all the way from New Jersey to St. Louis, several times a year. Every time we opened the box, we would find that *not one single cookie had broken*, and they are still the best cookies I have ever eaten. Words cannot express the joy my sister and I felt when the mail truck would arrive with that shoebox wrapped in brown paper. I have tried for years to duplicate those cookies, even with her original recipe, and they never tasted quite the same. Once I'd grown up and became a professional chef, I figured out what her secret ingredient is. There was a lot of love baked into those cookies! Even something as simple as cookies can be magical, if they are made with love. We have all felt of the awesome power of love and it is not to be underestimated.

Wizarding Levels Explained

Please read through these descriptions and decide which level of wizard you are. You should not consider the levels as any sort of restriction; they are just a guide to help find the right recipe for you. The recipes are written specifically for the types of wizards listed below and contain the right amount of knife work, methods or ingredients appropriate for that skill level. Eventually, you will gain more cooking skills and feel ready to move up to the next level, learning how to create magic in the kitchen along the way.

You will find the Wizarding Level just below the name of each recipe.

A **Novice Wizards** recipe is best for the youngest witches and wizards or those without much experience. The recipes are stated much more simply, with hints and suggestions built right in. Even a hopeless case should be able make a Novice recipe without destroying the house. Younger wizards would probably be suited to having an adult around to help, however. Don't be embarrassed if you are an adult Novice. Not everyone learns how to cook when they are young. You will catch right up with the rest of us in no time.

An **Initiate Wizards** recipe is for those with the basic cooking skills. Being able to read and understand a recipe, knowing how to use a sharp knife safely, and for younger wizards, permission to use the stove or oven and other kitchen equipment is suggested for this level. These recipes assume you know what boiling and chopping are and can do so safely, since they require a little more skill at the stove or with a knife than a Novice. Skilled pre-teens, teenagers and adults who don't know how to or have never tried to cook from scratch should feel comfortable with these recipes.

A Note to Adults: Please don't discourage underage wizards from trying these recipes! Just supervise them and help them with the things they are truly unable to do for themselves, like chopping hard foods with big knives or handling big pots full of boiling liquids. I was cooking four course meals for my family by the time I was ten years old, you might have a prodigy in your house, too!

A **Master Wizards** recipe is suited for those who cook often and are comfortable in a kitchen and with cooking from scratch. These recipes will have more advanced techniques and may involve cooking with wine or small amounts of spirits. There will be less in the way of helpful hints and the procedures will be more complicated. You don't need to be a professional chef to master these recipes; you just need to know your way around the kitchen. Most teenagers and adults can handle these, even if they don't cook all the time. Just pay attention to detail and you'll be fine.

Powerful Potions

Not for underage wizards!

Show your family you are a responsible person and wait until you're old enough. Also, no attempts at broom flying or driving of motor vehicles should be attempted after drinking these potions. The police take this very seriously, and so should you. No amount of fun is worth hurting yourself or someone else.

Kitchen Terms and Measurements

In this book, there are a few things you should know before starting. The abbreviation for a teaspoon is "tsp" and for a tablespoon, it is "Tbsp". An ounce can be either a liquid measure or solid weight. For our purposes, solid weight will be abbreviated to "oz" and liquid measures will be called for as "ounces" in these recipes.

Most importantly, enjoy yourself. This is meant to be fun, not a stressful nightmare. It's okay to make mistakes as long as you learn from them. If something goes wrong, throw it out and start over or order some Chinese take-out. As long as you tried and it was fun, who cares if one corner is a little burned? Nothing is learned by just reading a book, despite what anyone says. You have to practice, experiment, succeed and fail many, many times before you get really good at anything. There's nothing like the feeling you get when you realize something you used to think was so foreign and difficult becomes second nature.

Standard Measurements: Use measuring spoons and cups

A pinch =1/8 tsp or less

3 tsp = 1 Tbsp

4 Tbsp = ¼ cup

16 oz = 1 pound

Liquid measurements: Use liquid measuring cups

A pint of water weighs the same as a pound of a dry ingredient.

It helps to remember this old rhyme when you need liquid measures converted into solid weights, "a pint a pound, the world round"

2 Tbsp = 1 ounce

8 ounces = 1 cup

2 cups = 1 pint = 16 ounces

2 pints = 1 quart = 32 ounces

4 quarts = 1 gallon

Chop, cube or dice?

Chop: to cut into very small, but equal sized pieces.

Mince: to cut into tiny, evenly sized pieces.

Dice or cube: to cut into an even sided, square block.

Strips (or julienne): long rectangular pieces with squared edges

Rough chop: to cut into irregular sized pieces

Chunks: large irregular shaped pieces

How do I find:

Treacle: Usually found in the British foods aisle at International grocers, also called golden syrup. The black treacle is a too strongly flavored for our uses with this book. Some chain grocery stores will carry it if there are a lot of different cultures living in your area. Substitute molasses (not blackstrap) or dark corn syrup if need be.

Kidneys: Ask the person at the meat counter. If they don't have kidneys on display, they may have them in back or can very easily order some from their distributors.

Saffron: Again, try the international grocery stores, but please, please don't buy powdered or imitation saffron. The real thing will look like stiff orange-red threads and be more expensive than the imitations.

Roasting Chicken: Chickens are classified by the bird's age. Young, tender birds are preferred for broiling, roasting and frying, whereas older, bigger birds have to go in the stew pot. You'll be fine with anything between a stewing chicken to a tiny little Cornish hen. Those, by the way, are not a different breed; they are just the youngest, smallest, birds available. You can always ask your butcher to help you, that's why he's there.

Advice on Safe and Sanitary Cooking

First, common sense should be your most often used ingredient. If something seems like it might be a bad idea, it probably is. Sticking your hand into a food processor while it is running is a good example. There is no spell to re-grow fingers in this book, and trust me; it is not easy trying to explain why you did that to the doctors in the emergency room.

Kitchen Safety: Always use hot pads when handling pans. Sharp knives are also safer than dull ones. A dull knife needs a lot more force behind it to cut, and the chances of slipping and cutting yourself are greatly increased. Also, make no attempt to catch a knife that is dropped or falling; you will most likely cut yourself. There is not one knife in the world worth saving if you hurt yourself in the process. Let it fall to the floor, pick it up, inspect it for damage, wash it, and then go back to what you were doing. To keep cutting boards from slipping, place a clean, damp towel underneath and make sure it isn't wobbly.

Sanitation in the Kitchen: Serving undercooked or spoiled food is not only unappetizing; it can make people very sick. If you are not sure if something is fully cooked, don't eat it until you can get a more experienced wizard to check it for you. A good recipe will tell you how to check for doneness, but it's always best to be positive about these things before proceeding. Food poisoning is no joke and can lead to an embarrassing trip to the hospital for all parties involved. You will never have another willing dinner guest if word gets out that you are poisoning people. Your kitchen, equipment, ingredients and your hands must be as clean as possible. Immediately wash any tools, hands, knives and cutting boards after coming in contact with raw meats or seafood. Do not re-use any equipment without washing it thoroughly first. This is called cross contamination and should be avoided at all times. When in doubt, wash on the side of caution.

Do your homework: Take the time to read every recipe through twice to ensure that you have everything you'll need and that you clearly understand the procedures given and can visualize the desired result of the recipe. Another very important part of being a good magician is what chefs call *mise en place* which is French for "everything in place." This means that all the ingredients for each stage of the recipe are washed, trimmed, measured, cut up and close at hand. This prevents running back and forth looking for the next item to add to the dish while trying to cook at the same time. Walking away from boiling pots, sautéing meats or turning your back on the stove at any time should also be avoided.

The Bottom Line: Organization, safety, cleanliness and attention to detail are vital to becoming a master magician in the kitchen. It's usually the sloppy, scatterbrained and overly ambitious folks that turn out food that is definitely un-magical and sometimes dangerous. The best kitchen wizards will leave no trace of themselves, only wonderful memories, warm feelings and full tummies. You ought to think logically about changing recipes, too. Certainly there is always room for personal tastes and variations, but keep your wits about you, and think of what the people you are cooking for will enjoy, not just your personal preferences.

Foods for Feasting

Having friends over to celebrate is one of life's greatest joys. Since the beginning of history, people have gathered together at the end of harvests, to mark the changing of seasons, to welcome new beginnings and to say goodbye. These recipes are simple, yet will give your guests the illusion that you slaved away in the kitchen for days on end.

Bouillabaisse, page 14

Roasted Pumpkin-Cider Soup, page 16

Cornish Pasties, page 17

Wizard's Pie, page 19

Fish and Chips, page 20

Lamp Chops with Minted Port Wine sauce, page 22

Beef Stroganoff, page 23

Beef Bourguignon, page 25

Steak and Kidney Pie, page 26

Bouillabaisse

Master Wizards

Serves 4

This zesty tomato and fish stew is famous the world over. Cast a spell over your family on a cold night with this concoction and watch as everyone relaxes and comes together. The TV will be forgotten and work stress will melt away as the aroma reaches their noses. To serve this in the classic French style, you can garnish it with a spicy garlic mayonnaise called rouille on a crouton. Rouille can be made by adding some garlic paste and a good pinch of cayenne pepper to a spoonful of plain mayonnaise and mixing it well. Spread it on a toasted slice of French bread and launch it into the soup.

1 pound fresh Cod or other firm, mild white fish, cut into 2 inch cubes

12 medium sized raw shrimp, peeled and deveined

12 littleneck or other small clams

12 Mussels

1 orange, zested and juiced

1 lemon, zested and juiced

1 lime, zested and juiced

1 large yellow onion, chopped

3 Tbsp chopped garlic

16 oz canned plain diced tomatoes

½ cup dry white wine

1 qt fish or vegetable stock (look in the soup aisle at the store)

1 Tbsp thyme leaves

2 pieces star anise

2 Tbsp chopped flat leaf parsley

½ tsp cayenne pepper, more if you like spicier foods.

½ tsp saffron (please don't bother with anything but real saffron, skip it if need be.)

Olive oil for cooking

First, rinse your clams and mussels in cold running water for about ten minutes to flush out any sand then drain and keep very cold until ready to use. Do not use any clams or mussels that are open before cooking. They must be very tightly closed and have no strong smell or they are not safe to eat. Then, dice your onion and garlic, and set them aside separately. Use a citrus zester to get all the zest of your fruit, mix up the zests and set aside. Juice the remaining fruit into a small bowl and pick out any seeds. Chop your herbs, peel your shrimp, lightly season your fish with salt & pepper, and have everything else ready to go.

Heat a 2 quart pot over medium heat. Add enough oil to cover the bottom of the pan. Cook the onions until they start to soften, stirring often. Then add the garlic, herbs, pepper, saffron, citrus zest and star anise. When the garlic starts to give up its aroma, add the tomatoes, citrus juices and stock, stir to mix and simmer for 20 minutes.

When the broth is almost done simmering, heat up a large sauté pan and add enough oil to coat the bottom of the pan. Heat until the oil is hot but not smoking. Add the fish pieces and the clams first, since they need the most time to cook, turning the fish often so it is evenly cooked on all sides. When the fish is close to being fully cooked, it will start to flake and have an opaque appearance. At this time you want to add the shrimp and mussels, cooking them for just a few moments to get them started. Now remove the pan from the stovetop and add the white wine. It will let off a cloud of steam and the alcohol in the wine will vaporize. Return the pan to the stove and cover with a lid for a couple minutes or until the clams and mussels have all opened and the shrimp and fish are fully cooked and firm. Find the star anise in the broth and pick them out before serving. They are hard and inedible, like a cinnamon stick, and shouldn't make their way into the bowls.

Serve by placing 4 each of the clams, mussels and shrimp in each bowl and adding a few pieces of fish so every bowl has the same amounts. Ladle the hot broth over the seafood, sprinkle with the parsley and serve immediately.

Roasted Pumpkin-Cider Soup

Initiate Wizards

Serves 4-6

Rumor has it that this soup is actually an old witches' recipe for a warming potion. A bellyful of this before going outdoors in the winter will keep you toasty for sure! It takes a while to make, but is absolutely worth it. The kind of pumpkin you use to carve jack o' lanterns is not the same as the type you can eat. Look for smaller "eating" pumpkins near the squashes and other gourds at the grocery store. If they don't have them, try a local farmer's market. Sadly, most pumpkins are only harvested and brought to market in the fall. You can make this soup with Butternut squash if you need to. You will need a food processor or a blender to make this recipe. Very young wizards should not use sharp, whirly devices without adult supervision. They may also need help cutting the vegetables since carrots and pumpkins are a lot tougher than most veggies.

One 6-8 pound sugar or eating pumpkin, quartered, seeds and guts removed.

½ stick of butter

¼ cup brown sugar

1 large yellow onion, cut into medium sized pieces

6 garlic cloves, skin on if possible

3 carrots cut into medium sized pieces

1 green apple, peeled, cored and quartered

7-8 cups chicken or vegetable stock

2 cups apple cider

1 tsp ground ginger

½ tsp ground mace

1 small tub sour cream

Salt and pepper

Heat your oven to 350 degrees. Do all your chopping and cutting first, and have everything else measured and ready for when you'll need it. Place the pumpkin pieces in a large roasting pan and rub with the butter, then sprinkle with brown sugar. Arrange the carrots, onion, garlic and apple around the pumpkin. Lightly season everything by sprinkling salt and pepper onto the veggies. Pour 2 cups of the stock around the veggies and cover pan(s) with foil. Roast for about 1 ½ to 2 hours until the pumpkin and other veggies are fully cooked and squashy. Let cool a little before scooping the pumpkin flesh off the rind and squeeze the garlic out of its skins. Puree all of this in a food processor or blender until smooth, in batches if needed. Thin it out a little with stock if you need to.

Warning: Don't overload machines like food processors and blenders with thick foods, the machine will go crazy and try to eat your hand or blow itself up. Older machines are especially cranky. If it starts making weird sounds, stop the machine, unplug it and remove some of the contents, wait a few minutes to let the motor cool, plug it back in and try again. Once everything is pureed, put it in a large pot and whisk in the cider. Adjust the thickness with the remaining stock, and then add the mace and ginger. Bring to a boil, stirring often and then simmer 10 minutes to let the flavors blend. Taste and season with more salt and pepper to your liking. Garnish with a nice dollop of sour cream.

Cornish Pasties

Initiate Wizards

Serves 4

Cornwall is rumored to be the homeland the famous witch Morgan Le Fay. These clever little pocket sandwiches are a magic trick in their own right. It's like having a steak dinner with veggies and potato, all wrapped up to go. Usually served for lunches, pasties travel well and can be eaten with one hand, keeping your wand arm free in case of a dragon attack! These go beautifully with a cup of soup or just some cheese and fruit.

1 package of 2 refrigerated prepared pie crusts

1 pound beef sirloin cut into very small cubes

2 large russet potatoes, scrubbed, peeled and cut into very small cubes

½ yellow onion, cut into small pieces

3 carrots, scrubbed, peeled and cut into very small cubes

¼ cup steak sauce

Salt and pepper

2 eggs

Get all your scrubbing, peeling and cutting done first. The veggies and meat need to be very small so they will be fully cooked inside the pasty without the crust burning. Then, in a large bowl, mix all the veggies and meat together with the steak sauce and a little salt and pepper. Preheat the oven to the temperature recommended on the pie crust package. Unroll the pie crusts on a flat surface. Take the eggs and crack them into a small bowl with a little cold water and beat with a fork. Cut each pie crust in half. Now you have 4 pieces of dough. On one half of each piece, place a mound of the meat and veggie mixture, leaving a little room around the edges. Brush a little of the egg mixture on the edges of each piece with either a pastry brush or your fingers. Flop the other half of each piece of dough over the filling and press firmly around the edges to seal the pasty. Brush the tops of each pasty with the remaining egg mixture and cut a tiny X on top with a knife to let the steam escape. Place the pasties on a cookie sheet and bake at 350 degrees in the center of the oven for 45-50 minutes. Let the pasties cool for a few minutes before you serve them, since the filling will be extremely hot!

Wizard's Pie

Novice Wizards

Serves 6

Wizards are busy people, what with dragons attacking villages, people asking for love charms, and evil always lurking about. They need a hearty meal that doesn't take too long to make. Young wizards will like the cheesy, crusty potatoes and the vegetables are so well hidden you'd think they were invisible! Serve with some salad or fresh fruit for a complete meal that will keep you on your feet when facing goblin hordes.

You will need a 9 inch pie pan for this recipe.

6 servings instant mashed potatoes prepared according to directions and set aside

2 cups frozen peas and carrots or other mixed veggies

1 pound very lean ground beef

¼ cup yellow onion, chopped

1 tsp chopped garlic

4 ounces tomato paste

1 packet instant onion soup

½ cup hot water

2 tsp steak sauce

Salt and pepper, as needed.

½ cup shredded cheddar cheese

Make the potatoes first, you want them ready before this pie is assembled, and have everything else measured and close at hand. Then, in a deep skillet, cook the ground beef with the garlic, stirring to break up any big chunks of beef, until it is fully cooked and browned. Drain any excess fat from the meat, and then add the water and onion soup packet, stirring well to mix up the soup. Add the tomato paste and steak sauce, and then stir them in. Add the peas and carrots, and then simmer for about 5 minutes to cook the veggies. Taste the mixture, adding salt and pepper if needed. Turn off the heat and let the meat minute cool off a little bit. Next, turn your oven on to 375 degrees. Pour the meat and vegetable mixture into the pan and spread it out to the sides. Take the potatoes and drop by spoonfuls all across the top of the meat, spreading it into an even layer. Leave little peaks and swirls in the potatoes to add visual appeal. Place the pan in the oven and bake for about 10 minutes, or until the potatoes are golden brown and crusty. Sprinkle with the cheese and return to the oven until the cheese is melted. Let the pie rest about 10 minutes before serving, then spoon up a plateful and enjoy.

Fish and Chips

Master Wizards

Serves 4

Every wizard's castle has at least one vat of boiling oil ready to dump on invaders, but they are also handy for a fish fry or two in the peaceful times. Deep frying on the stove is quite manageable with a little patience, a deep heavy pot and a candy thermometer, but you must be *very* careful around hot oil. It takes a little practice to keep the oil at exactly 375 degrees on the stovetop without an automatic thermostat like you find on an electric deep fryer. Decide for yourself, but I personally prefer the ease of using an electric countertop deep fryer.

For the fish:

2 cups flour, plus 1 cup extra flour, seasoned with salt and pepper, kept separate.

1 egg

½ can of beer

¼ tsp salt

¼ cup milk

3 pounds fresh firm fleshed white fish such as Cod, Flounder or Haddock

Have the frying oil heating up while you make the batter for the fish. Set your fryer to 375 degrees, or if you are using the stovetop method, you will have to keep adjusting the heat to keep the oil from smoking and keep it as close to 375 degrees as possible. Clip your candy thermometer to the pot to tell you how hot the oil is, Frying in oil that is below 360 degrees will not get the batter crispy and it will start to absorb the oil, getting all soggy and greasy. Using two bowls combine the dry ingredients in one bowl and the wet ingredients into the other. Whisk together the wet ingredients, and then slowly add to the dry ingredients, stirring gently until no lumps appear. Cut the fish into desired size and dredge lightly with the seasoned flour. Then dunk each piece in the batter, shake off the excess and gently drop into the hot oil. Fry about 3- 5 minutes, turning periodically until golden brown and crisp. Drain on paper towels in a 250 degree oven until served. Serve hot with tartar sauce, malt vinegar and ketchup, along with some hot, crispy chips.

For the Chips:

6 Large russet potatoes, scrubbed and peeled

Oil for frying (see above)

Scrub and peel your potatoes, then cut them into ½ inch thick rounds. Soak the cut potatoes in cold water for at least 30 minutes to release any excess starch. If serving fried fish with your chips, cook it during the water soaking time for the chips, so everything is hot and fresh at close to the same time. The fish will stay hot in the oven while you're cooking chips, but the chips must be served right away or they will get soggy and gross. Drain and dry the potatoes on towels before blanching so they don't spit at you when they go into the oil. Have the oil heated to 375 degrees, and skim out any "batter crunchies" that may have accumulated when frying the fish. The proper cooking of chips is a two step process. First you will blanch the chips by frying in the hot oil for 5 minutes, then draining and cooling the potatoes for 10 minutes. Then take them back to the fryer and fry them again another 5 minutes or until they are crispy and brown. Spread on paper towels and season immediately with salt.

Lamb Chops with Minted Port Wine Sauce

Master Wizards

Serves: 4

You may find yourself infatuated with this dish, but be assured there are no sneaky love charms hidden in this recipe, it's just really good! The trick is the long, slow cooking of the sauce. Sweet and complex, it compliments lamb perfectly and dresses it up quite a bit more than plain old mint jelly. Serve along with some mashed potatoes and fresh steamed vegetables.

2 Frenched racks of lamb, about 6 -8 bones per rack. (Frenched means the bones are trimmed and cleaned, the butcher can do it for you)

½ bottle of inexpensive port wine

1 cup real mint jelly, the kind with the mint leaves still in it.

1 shallot, minced

1 Tbsp chopped garlic

1 Tbsp butter

Montreal steak seasoning (comes premixed in shakers in the spice aisle)

Vegetable oil

Mint sprigs for garnish

First thing you'll need to do is start the sauce. Melt the butter in a saucepan over medium heat and add the shallot and garlic. Cook until they begin to take on a little color. Add the port and the jelly, and then whisk it all together until smooth. Lower the heat to a bare simmer and let the sauce slowly thicken as the liquids evaporate, concentrating the flavors, as well as cooking out all the alcohol. This could take up to 45 minutes since the sugar in the jelly will simply burn if you tried this over high heat. Stir the sauce occasionally and adjust the heat if you need to. You want the sauce to be shiny, with a deep color and thick enough to coat the back of a spoon. While the sauce is simmering, you can prepare the lamb.

You'll want to try and time this so the sauce and lamb are done at the same time. Usually a 30 minute head start for the sauce is enough. Season the lamb racks lightly with the steak seasoning. Put a large skillet on to heat on medium high. Add just enough oil to coat the pan, and then sear each rack on all sides. You don't need to worry about cooking them to a certain temperature; you just want a nice crust on the meat. Then, transfer the lamb to a pan and finish cooking it in a 375 degree oven for about 15-20 minutes for medium rare. Use your meat thermometer to test for doneness. Medium rare is around 140 degrees, medium is 150-160 degrees and anything more than that will be medium well (170-180 degrees) to well done (anything over 180 degrees). Remove the lamb and place on a cutting board to rest for about 5 minutes. If you cut into the lamb right away, all the juices will run out. After the meat has rested and the sauce is ready, cut each rack into separate chops. Each person should get 3 or 4 chops depending on the size of the racks. To serve, Fan out the chops on a plate with the bones together in the center, then spoon the sauce across the meatiest part of each chop and drizzle a little more around the plate for presentation.

Beef Stroganoff

Master Wizards

Serves 4

This hearty beef dish could make even the evil Russian wizard Rasputin feel warm and happy. This is so much better than the ground beef boxed dinner kind of stroganoff you may have had, and doesn't really take that much longer to make. Serve some vegetables or a salad along with this to make for a complete meal.

1 ½ pound beef sirloin, cut into ½ inch by 1 inch strips

1 large yellow onion, peeled, cut in half and sliced about ¼ inch thick

10 white button mushrooms, scrubbed and sliced ¼ inch thick

1 ounce vodka or red wine

1 tsp Dijon mustard

1 ½ cups sour cream

Tabasco sauce

Salt and pepper

3 Tbsp coarsely chopped flat leaf parsley

1 package wide egg noodles

Butter or margarine

Fill a deep pot with water, bring it to almost a boil and add some salt to season the water. You'll want to time cooking the noodles so they are ready at the same time as the meat. Keep the water hot and ready, but wait to boil the noodles until the time is right. Do all your cutting and chopping first to have everything ready. You could be cooking the onions and mushrooms while you are cutting up the meat, if you wanted to save a little time.

In a large deep skillet, melt a large pat of butter over medium heat. Add the onions and cook them slowly until they are limp and starting to brown, then add the mushrooms and cook until they are soft. Add the meat and a little salt and pepper. Cook the meat with the mushrooms and onions until fully cooked and well browned. Add the vodka or wine and the mustard to the juices in the pan, stirring to mix. You should now turn the heat down and stir often to cool it down, and then stir in the sour cream. If you add sour cream to a really hot pan, it will curdle or separate and not look very appetizing. Add the sour cream and a dash of Tabasco sauce. Don't worry, you won't taste any spiciness, but sauces made with dairy products magically taste better with a dash or two of Tabasco. Stir the sauce to mix in the sour cream completely. Taste the sauce and season with a little more salt and pepper if you need to. If the sauce is too thick and creamy for you, thin it out with a little milk, stirring it over low heat. Serve by pouring the meat over the buttered noodles in a deep dish and sprinkle with the parsley.

Beef Bourguignon

Master Wizards

Serves 4

Be careful who you feed this to; they may fall in love with you over this wine-rich beef delight. This should be served with either boiled new potatoes, or over buttered egg noodles. This dish can be complimented by a simple green salad, dressed with your favorite vinaigrette to offset the richness of the sauce.

2 pounds beef stew meat, cut into ½ inch cubes.

1 Tbsp all purpose flour

½ yellow onion, chopped

2 Tbsp garlic, chopped

2 carrots cut into very small cubes

2 tsp fresh thyme leaves

1 tsp fresh rosemary leaves, chopped fine

1 bay leaf

2 Tbsp vegetable oil

Salt and pepper

½ bottle of red wine

1 c beef stock

Cornstarch, if needed

First thing is to get all your chopping done and have the other ingredients measured and ready. Then, in a deep pot, heat the oil over medium heat. Place the meat in a bowl and toss it with the flour, coating it evenly. Add the meat, onions, garlic and carrots to the pot, then season with a little salt and pepper. Cook until the meat is well browned and the onions and garlic are getting soft. Carefully add the red wine and stock, giving the pot a good stirring. Lower the heat to a steady simmer. Mix in the herbs and bay leaves. Let simmer uncovered for at least 2 hours. Stir it up once in a while to keep things from sticking to the bottom of the pot. You want the amount of liquid to reduce by half its volume. If the sauce is still thin after 2 hours, mix a tablespoon of cornstarch with a little cold water and stir it in. The sauce will thicken after a few minutes and a little stirring. Make sure you time the cooking of your noodles or potatoes so they are still hot when the beef is ready. To serve, pour the meat and sauce over the potatoes or noodles and tuck in.

Steak and Kidney Pie

Master Wizards

Serves 4

This dish is much better than the usual witches' pies full of lost children! You don't have to add the kidneys if you don't want to, but it never hurts to try new things. If you do decide to omit the kidneys, double the amount of sirloin and call it steak and mushroom pie. Serve with mashed potatoes and vegetables for a full meal.

1 sheet frozen puff pastry dough, thawed.

1 pound beef sirloin cut into 1 inch cubes

1 Tbsp all purpose flour

12 fresh white button mushrooms, scrubbed and sliced ¼ inch thick

½ yellow onion, chopped

1 tsp Worcestershire sauce

1 Tbsp fresh thyme leaves

1 Tbsp fresh chopped parsley

2 ounces sherry or red wine

2 ounces beef stock or water

2 oz butter

1 egg beaten with 1 Tbsp water

Get the cutting and chopping done first, so you can prepare this pie all at once. Preheat your oven to 425 degrees. Then heat a large skillet over high heat and add the butter. In a bowl, toss the beef cubes with some salt and pepper and the flour to coat lightly and evenly. Add the beef to the pan and cook, stirring often, until the meat is about halfway finished cooking. Turn the heat down to medium and add mushrooms, herbs and onions to the pan. Continue cooking and stirring often until the mushrooms and onions are cooked and the beef is done. If you are adding kidneys, do so at this point. The kidneys only need a very brief time in the pan. Cooking organ meats too long, or with too high of a temperature will turn them rubbery and not very appetizing. Cook the kidneys just enough to firm them up and get a little color on them; they will cook more in the oven. Next thing is to make the sauce. The flour you tossed the beef in will absorb the liquids you are adding to the pan and will form a thickened gravy for the pie. First, add the sherry or wine, then the stock and the Worcestershire sauce and stir it all well to combine. Let this simmer a few more minutes to thicken while you stir often. When the sauce is thickened, pour the entire contents of the pan into your pie dish. Brush the edges of the pan with the beaten egg, so the dough has something to cling to. Then, take your thawed puff pastry sheet, roll it out a little bit with a rolling pin, and drape it across the top of the pie so it has enough extra around the edges to seal it. Firmly press the dough all around the edge of the pan to seal it and cut off any excess. Brush the dough evenly with the beaten eggs. Cut an X in the center of the pie for a steam vent and place it in the oven. Bake for 10 minutes at 425, then turn the oven down to 400 and bake for 15 -20 minutes or until the crust is puffed, crisp and brown. Cool 10 minutes before cutting. If you have dough scraps left over, you can use them to decorate your pie. Before it goes into the oven, cut the leftover dough into shapes and stick it to the pie by laying the shapes on the pie after it has been brushed with the egg. Then brush the pieces you just added with a little more of the egg mixture and bake.

Conjuring for a Crowd

Unless you can turn coal into gold, or are good friends with a leprechaun, sometimes stretching your food dollar is necessary. These recipes are either very inexpensive to make, make use of leftovers, or make so much food that you can feed a large group cheaply.

Scotch Broth, page 30

Crumpets, page 30

Sourdough Hotcakes, page 32

Toad in Hole, page 33

Chicken and Ham Pie, page 34

Welsh Rarebit, page 36

Roasted Chicken, page 37

Lamb Stew, page 38

Corned Beef and Cabbage, page 40

Scotch Broth

Novice Wizards

Serves 4

This simple but strong broth is the Scottish witches' answer to chicken noodle soup. It can help you get over a cold, not to mention being easy to make and delicious. You could use beef or chicken, but then it wouldn't be as authentic as using lamb.

6 cups water

1 ½ pounds lamb shoulder meat, trimmed of fat and cut into 1 inch cubes

½ cup pearl barley

1 yellow onion, peeled and chopped

1 carrot, scrubbed and cut into pieces

1 stalk celery, washed and cut into small pieces

Salt and pepper

2 Tbsp chopped parsley

First do all the washing, peeling and cutting so everything is measured and ready when you start cooking. Add everything to the pot and season it with salt and pepper. Bring to a simmer for 10 minutes. Using a ladle, skim off any stuff that floats to the top. Simmer another hour and a half, adding a little water if too much evaporation occurs. Taste the broth to see if it needs more salt and pepper and serve hot in mugs.

Crumpets

Initiate Wizards

Makes 10 crumpets

The original "English" muffin! Serve to guests you may suspect of being fairies in disguise. Legend has it that if you give fairies some bread, they will bless your house.

You will need some 3 inch wide metal rings to cook the crumpets in. If you don't have a set of crumpet rings at home (who does?) simply cut the tops and bottoms off empty tuna fish cans, remove the labels and wash thoroughly before using.

1 packet active dry yeast

½ tsp sugar

2 Tbsp warm water (110 to 115 degrees)

1 cup all purpose flour

¼ tsp salt

½ cup milk

1 egg

1 Tbsp melted butter

Nonstick pan spray, as needed

In a small bowl, dissolve the yeast and sugar in the warm water for about 3 minutes, stir and set it in a warm place for about 5 minutes or until the yeast is bubbly.

Sift the flour and salt into a large bowl and make a well in the center. Add the yeast mixture, the milk and egg. Beat everything together vigorously and then add the melted butter and beat until a smooth, soft batter forms. Drape a kitchen towel loosely over the bowl and let the dough rise for an hour in a warm place, or until doubled in volume. When the dough is ready, coat the bottom of a heavy bottomed skillet with the nonstick spray and put it on the stove over medium high heat. Spray the inside of each ring, and then place them in the pan. Drop about 1 ½ tablespoons of batter into each ring and let bubble and cook until the bottoms are lightly browned. Remove the rings with tongs and flip over each crumpet and cook the other side. Finished crumpets can be kept hot in a 200 degree oven covered loosely with foil while the rest of the batch is cooking. When ready to eat, split each crumpet and toast.

Sourdough Hotcakes

Initiate Wizards

Serves 4 -6 depending on size

These are far more magical than any other hotcakes you may encounter. Tangy, light and delicious, just make sure they don't levitate off the table! Working with yeast is a balance between chemistry and timing. It's not hard, and the results will spoil you forever against boxed pancake mix.

Step One:

2 ½ Tbsp active dry yeast

½ cup warm water (105 to 115 degrees)

1 ½ cups warm milk (105 to 115 degrees)

3 Tbsp unsalted butter, melted

2 cups all purpose flour

3 Tbsp sugar

Mix the yeast and warm water in a bowl and let stand until the yeast is dissolved and bubbly, about 5 minutes. Whisk in the warm milk and the melted butter. In a large bowl, mix the flour and sugar together, then pour the wet ingredients into the flour mixture and gently whisk together until just combined. Cover the bowl tightly with plastic wrap and leave in a warm place for one hour. Let the mixture increase in volume by half and start to bubble. Unwrap the bowl and stir the batter to deflate the bubbles. Cover with plastic again and let the bowl rest overnight at room temperature. You can refrigerate the batter overnight as well, but let it warm up to room temperature before starting step two.

Step Two:

2 large eggs, lightly beaten

1 tsp salt

Nonstick pan spray, as needed

Stir to deflate the batter and mix in the eggs and salt. Preheat your griddle and turn the oven to 200 degrees for keeping finished hotcakes warm. The griddle is hot enough when a drop of water spits at you. Spray the griddle with a little nonstick spray if you need to, then drop ¼ cup of the batter for each hotcake. The batter may seem to be runny at first, but don't worry about it, they will puffy and wonderful when they are done cooking. When bubbles are breaking frequently on the surface and the edges are cooked, flip the hotcake over and cook the other side. Serve hot with butter, maple syrup, honey or whatever you like.

Toad in Hole

Novice Wizards

Serves 4

Toads have always been a witch's favorite ingredient in potions, but eating them for breakfast really isn't a good idea. Breakfast sausage stands in for the toads in this dish. Warm some pancake syrup to serve alongside for a supreme brunch that will disappear right before your eyes. You will need a deep baking dish to make this recipe.

1 cup all-purpose flour

2 eggs

1 cup milk

½ tsp salt

½ tsp black pepper

1 package pre-cooked breakfast sausage links

In a large bowl, beat the eggs and salt together with a whisk until frothy. Slowly sift in the flour, a little bit at a time, beating constantly. Add the milk in a thin stream and beat until the mixture is smooth and creamy. Cover and chill the batter for at least an hour. Preheat the oven to 400 degrees. Arrange the sausages in a layer in a buttered baking dish, keeping a little space between each one. Stir up the batter once again to check for lumps. Then pour the batter evenly over the sausages and bake for 30- 40 minutes or until the batter has puffed up and is crisp and brown. Serve at once.

Chicken and Ham Pie

Novice Wizards

Serves 4-6

It's not four and twenty blackbirds, it's chicken! This is a nice family supper, and it is easy to make. If you have leftover cooked chicken from another dish, use that instead of cooking more. Witches and wizards are known for their resourcefulness, plus it's horrible to waste food. Even an inexperienced wizard can make this dish easily, using canned soup and prepared pie crusts.

1 package of 2 refrigerated prepared pie crusts

1 can condensed cream of chicken soup, plus water to fill ¼ of the can

1 cup frozen peas

2 pounds raw chicken breast, rinsed, trimmed of fat and cut into small cubes

1 thick ham steak, trimmed of fat and cut into small cubes

2 Tbsp vegetable oil

2 cups dry beans or rice from the pantry to act as pie weights

Aluminum foil

1 egg beaten with a little water

First thing you'll need to do is pre-bake your bottom pie crust so it won't get soggy. Preheat your oven to 375 degrees. Lightly butter the pie pan and place one crust in the pan and pat it down along the sides and edges, so it is smooth and flat. Poke it gently all over with a fork. Cover the dough with foil and pat it down, so the foil completely covers the dough. Pour your dry beans or rice to make an even layer across the bottom of the pan. Bake the crust for 20 minutes, then remove it from the oven and carefully remove the beans and foil. Bake another 5-10 minutes until golden brown, then take it out of the oven to cool while you make the pie filling. Don't turn off the oven yet, because you'll need it again soon. While the bottom crust is cooking, you should be doing all your cutting and measuring for the rest of the recipe.

Put a large skillet on the stove and turn the heat up to medium high. Add the oil to the pan and let it heat up before adding the chicken. When you add the chicken, it will sizzle and you need to stir it with a wooden spoon so it doesn't stick to the pan. Sauté the chicken until it is completely cooked and starting to brown. You will know the chicken is done when the pieces are firm when pressed with the spoon. Lower the heat and add the soup, water, peas and ham cubes. Stir all this up to mix well and then turn off the heat. Let the chicken mixture cool off about 10 minutes so it doesn't steam too much inside the pie, because that makes the crusts tough. Fill the bottom crust with the chicken and ham filling, spreading it around evenly. Brush the edges of the bottom crust with the beaten egg. Take the top crust and unroll it across the rest of the pie. Pinch the edges tightly together to seal in all the filling. Poke a few holes in the top crust for steam vents. Take a little more foil and wrap the edges of the pie to keep them from overcooking. Bake the pie about 20 -30 minutes or until the top crust is golden brown and crisp. Remove the foil covering the edges about 15 minutes after putting the pie in the oven. Let it cool a little before serving with a nice big salad and boiled potatoes.

Welsh Rarebit

Master Wizards

Serves 2-4

Instead of pulling a rabbit out of your hat, try making some rarebit instead. It will impress your guests and it so very delicious. You can also make what is known as a "Horseshoe Sandwich" by laying warmed, thinly sliced ham, turkey or roast beef over the toast and covering it with the rarebit. Have some fruit and salad on the table, too.

3 slices of Texas toast style bread per person

3 Tbsp butter

1 pound shredded sharp cheddar cheese

1 tsp cornstarch

¾ cup of any kind of beer or stout, at room temperature

2 egg yolks, beaten

Tabasco or other hot sauce

Worcestershire sauce

½ tsp Dijon mustard

Make a double boiler by setting a large metal or glass bowl over a pot of simmering water. Melt the butter, and whisk in the cheese, cornstarch, egg yolks and the beer. It will look like a sloppy mess at first, but with low heat and lots of stirring, it will be velvety smooth. You may have to remove the bowl from the over the water a few times and let it cool down if it starts to bubble. Season it with the mustard, one dash of Tabasco and two dashes of Worcestershire, stirring constantly to keep it smooth. Don't let the rarebit cook too long or get too hot, because it will get grainy. While the sauce is cooking, toast the bread and cut in half diagonally. Lay 6 of the triangles in a row on each plate, points facing the same way. Pour the rarebit over the toast on each plate and serve.

Roasted Chicken

Novice Wizards

Serves 4

Use caution! The smells coming from your kitchen when you make this might draw the whole neighborhood to your door. Enchanted by the aroma, they will eventually return to their homes, but probably not until they get some chicken so you might want to make two! Serve this along with some veggies and potatoes for a well rounded supper.

1 medium sized roasting chicken, about 6-8 pounds

1 yellow onion, cut into chunks

6 garlic gloves, cut lengthways

1 lemon, quartered

¼ stick butter, softened at room temperature

1 -2 sticks of fresh rosemary

8 fresh sage leaves

8 -10 stems of fresh thyme

Salt and pepper

Butcher's twine

A meat thermometer

First thing you should do is get all the cutting done so you have everything ready when you need it. Heat your oven to 400 degrees and lower the rack to the 2nd from bottom position. Start by rinsing off your chicken to remove any juices. Check the cavity for giblets and rinse the inside of the chicken. Pat it dry with paper towels. Cut off any hanging fat and the wing tips (the pointy, inedible bits) with kitchen shears or a knife. Rub the butter all over and inside the bird. Gently lift the skin on the breast and rub some butter under there, too. Be careful, because you do not want to tear or remove the skin. Take a few garlic pieces and some of the herbs and tuck under the skin, pushing them as far back towards the wings as possible. Smooth the skin back over the breast. Stuff the cavity of the bird with the lemon, onion, remaining garlic and herbs. Season with salt and pepper and tie up the chicken with some butcher's twine. All you want to do is tie the legs and wings to the body so they are snug up against the rest of the bird during cooking. It doesn't matter how pretty it looks, since you'll remove the twine before serving, anyway. Place the trussed bird (careful, he's all buttery and slippery now) in a roasting pan and cook 1 hour for every 4 pounds of chicken, or 15 minutes per pound. To test for doneness; stick the meat thermometer halfway into the thigh, the chicken will be ready to eat when the thermometer reads 180 degrees. Take it out of the oven and let it rest for about 10 minutes. Take all the stuff out of the cavity with a long spoon and throw it out. Get someone to help you carve the bird into breast and leg pieces or just tear it apart with your fingers, but be careful, it's still really hot!

Lamb Stew

Initiate Wizards

Serves 6 - 8

Witches and wizards are notorious for gazing into their bubbling cauldrons. Maybe they were making this stew and were hoping it would be ready soon. Yes, it takes time, but it is superb and should be tried at least once! All your dining companions will probably fall asleep after this rich and satisfying meal, but I promise there is no sleeping potion hidden in the recipe. This recipe is easily made with beef stew meat, if you don't like or can't get lamb. You will also need a heavy bottomed, deep pot for this recipe.

3 pounds lamb stew meat (just ask your butcher to cut up leg meat if they don't have stew meat already offered.)

4 large russet potatoes, scrubbed, peeled and cut into medium size chunks

2 large yellow onions, chopped

2 large carrots, scrubbed, peeled and cut into medium size chunks

2 parsnips, scrubbed, peeled and cut into medium size chunks

½ can tomato paste

2 Tbsp thyme

1 Tbsp rosemary

2 bay leaves

½ cup red wine

2 Tbsp vegetable oil

¼ c all purpose flour

1 qt beef stock

Salt and pepper

Start by cleaning and cutting all your vegetables and lamb and have everything else measured and ready. In a large bowl, toss the flour and lamb together to evenly dust the meat cubes. Season with a little salt and pepper. Heat your pot over high heat and add the oil. Place the meat, onions, potatoes, carrots and parsnips in the pot and stir a few times to prevent sticking. Once the meat is almost browned, add the tomato paste and mix it in well. Then, carefully add the wine and let it simmer until it nearly disappears. Stir with a wooden spoon to loosen any stuck pieces, since the flour will now start to act as a thickener. Add the stock and the herbs. Don't worry if it seems too thin, the liquid will evaporate over time. Once everything is well mixed up, add a little more salt and pepper then turn the heat to low and let the stew simmer for at least 2- 3 hours. Once the stew is ready, pick out the bay leaves. The longer this stew cooks, the better, but if you're hungrier than you are patient, 2 hours will do fine. If you do decide to go for the longer cooking time, stir the pot once in a while to make sure it's not burning or sticking to the bottom. If it gets really thick, add a little water. The best way to enjoy this stew is the old fashioned way, served inside a loaf of bread. Many bakeries and grocery stores sell "bread bowls" and they are easy to prepare, just cut a circle on the top and pull out the center, leaving at least a ¾ of an inch of bread and crust to hold in the stew.

Corned Beef and Cabbage

Initiate Wizards

Serves 6- 8

You don't have to save this for St Patrick's Day, it is good any time of year. The magic lies in the slow simmering of the meat to make it fork tender. This is another recipe where you may find uninvited guests on your doorstep once the smell gets out of the house. What can I say? It's magic. Note: Corned beef is a cured and then simmered beef brisket. Since most people cannot just go out and buy sodium nitrate (it's a special meat curing salt that shouldn't be handled by anyone but an expert butcher and generally is not for sale to the public, anyway), you will use a pre-cured but not cooked and not quite yet fully "corned" beef brisket. You will need 2 large pots for this recipe.

8-10 pound Corned Beef brisket with seasoning included (can be found in most chain grocery stores)

3 heads green cabbage

Caraway seed

Celery salt

Butter or margarine as needed, softened to room temperature

For Horseradish Sauce:

¼ cup sour cream, ¼ cup mayonnaise, 2 Tbsp or more prepared horseradish, and 2 dashes Worcestershire sauce, mixed together and chilled.

In one pot, place the brisket, seasoning packet and cold water, then turn up the heat and simmer it according to the directions on the package. Enjoy the heavenly aroma that will fill the house and make your stomach growl for the next few hours. Poke at the meat once in a while with a meat fork to test the tenderness. Some people like their corned beef a little firm to make it easier to slice, while others enjoy cooking it until it starts to positively melt and fall apart.

About half an hour before it's time to eat, fill the second large pot with water and add some salt. Cut each cabbage into quarters, leaving the stem attached so the leaves stay together. Drop the cabbage into boiling water, and cook uncovered for about 5 -10 minutes. The cabbage should be cooked, but not limp or soggy. Drain the cabbage quarters into a colander, then put the cabbage in a large baking dish and butter it and sprinkle with a little of the celery salt and caraway. Cover loosely with foil and keep warm in a 250 degree oven until the meat is ready to serve. Once the meat is finished, turn off the heat and pull the meat out with a meat fork and tongs onto a ready cutting board. Let it rest a few minutes then slice it across the grain with a long, sharp knife. The grain means the long strands you see running lengthways along the meat. You want to cut across to these strands or the meat will be stringy. You should also trim off any remaining fat at this time. Arrange the slices nicely on a serving plate and serve it with the cabbage and horseradish sauce. Having leftover corned beef is a real bonus if your family is smaller than the Weasleys. If kept well wrapped and refrigerated, you can use the leftovers in sandwiches or in corned beef hash for breakfast the next day. That reminds me…

Corned Beef Hash

Novice Wizards

Serves: depends on leftovers

Waste not, want not! There is a special reason this recipe is not listed in the table of contents. It's a bonus recipe for people like me (and you) who read every word of every book, even cookbooks. I have even read cookbooks under the covers with a flashlight!

This is great for breakfast with some eggs on the side or alone for a quick dinner.

Take any cold, leftover corned beef and chop it into small pieces. Find a few potatoes, peel them and cut them into little cubes. If you like onions, chop some up and toss them in, too. Cook the potatoes in a little vegetable oil over medium high heat until they start to turn brown and begin to soften up a little. Add the onion if you choose to, and cook until softened. Add the corned beef and cook until it starts to get crispy, flipping the hash over with a spatula once in a while. Season with salt and pepper or seasoning salt if you like it and serve hot.

Tricks for Treats

Sweets for the sweet! Witches and wizards are known to love candy and sweets, some even more than children. Remember the witch who lived in a gingerbread house? Case closed.

Rhubarb Crumble with Custard Sauce, page 44

Mince Pies, page 46

Nut Brittle, page 47

Homemade Strawberry Ice Cream, page 49

Pumpkin Punch, page 51

Caramel Apples, page 51

Chocolate Wands, page 53

Treacle Toffee, page 54

Trifle, page 55

Treacle Tart, page 57

Pumpkin Pie Pockets, page 58

Knickerbocker Glory, page 59

Rhubarb Crumble with Custard Sauce

Initiate Wizards

Serves 8

Rhubarb is a magical vegetable due to it's ability to look and taste like something else. It looks like red celery, has leaves like chard, but tastes like strawberries. That's amazing! The topping on this dessert forms crunchy little bits after it's cooked, and the batter bakes up nice and tender, almost like a coffeecake. Serve with ice cream or whipped cream. You can substitute strawberries or practically any fruit or berry for the rhubarb with this recipe, but you won't need to pre-cook them like you do the rhubarb. Have a glass baking dish buttered and ready for this recipe.

For the crumb topping:

½ cup sugar

6 Tbsp all purpose flour

¼ tsp salt

¼ tsp ground cinnamon

½ stick unsalted butter, cut into small pieces.

In a bowl, add all the crumb ingredients together and using a pastry cutter or two forks, smash up the butter into the flour and sugar to make a crumbly mixture and set aside until you need it.

For the crumble:

1 ¾ cups all purpose flour

2 tsp baking powder

½ tsp salt

¾ stick unsalted butter, softened until nearly melted

1 cup sugar plus 2 tablespoons extra

1 large egg

½ tsp vanilla extract

½ cup milk

2 pounds rhubarb stalks washed and cut into 1 inch pieces

First, melt 1/3 of the butter in a medium pan, then add the rhubarb and the 2 Tbsp of the sugar and cook over medium heat until the rhubarb has softened and the sugar has melted. Set aside to cool. In one bowl, mix the flour, baking powder and salt. In another, mix the butter, sugar, egg and vanilla. Whip either by hand or machine until fluffy, then gradually beat in the milk. Add the wet mixture to the dry ingredients and stir until moistened and smooth. Fold the rhubarb (or other fruit) into the batter gently and pour into the buttered baking dish. Sprinkle with the crumb topping and bake for 40 -45 minutes or until a toothpick inserted near the middle comes out clean. Let cool in the pan for at least 20 minutes before serving.

Custard Sauce (also known as Crème Anglaise)

1 ½ cup heavy cream

2 Tbsp sugar

3 egg yolks

½ vanilla bean, split

In a heavy saucepan, heat the cream and the vanilla bean until almost boiling. Carefully fish out the vanilla bean and scrape the remaining seeds into the milk with the back of a knife. In a bowl, whisk the egg yolks together with the sugar until pale and the sugar dissolves. Slowly add the hot milk while continuing to whisk the eggs, so the hot milk doesn't cook the eggs too quickly or you will get eggy lumps that will need to be strained out. Once the milk and eggs are mixed together, pour into the saucepan and return to the stove. Cook the custard sauce over medium heat, stirring constantly with a heatproof rubber spatula until thick and smooth. Serve hot or cold.

Mince Pies

Master Wizards

Makes 12 miniature tarts or 1 full size pie.

Mincemeat pies have a long history of being served for winter holidays, with some recipes dating back to medieval times. Making mincemeat the old fashioned way takes at least 3 weeks and uses beef suet or lard. That sounds like it would be greasy and 3 weeks is too long to wait for dessert, so unless you can time travel, use this simpler recipe. You will need muffin pans for making individual sized pies, or a 9 inch pie pan for one large one.

¼ stick unsalted butter

4 cups seedless raisins

2 cups dried currants

1 cup coarsely chopped almonds, optional if you are allergic

1 cup chopped candied cherries or any other candied/dried fruit you like

1 Tbsp orange zest

1 Tbsp lemon zest

6 Granny Smith apples, peeled, cored and diced into small cubes

1 ½ cups sugar

1 tsp ground nutmeg

1 tsp ground allspice

1 tsp ground cinnamon

½ tsp ground cloves

2 cups Brandy

4 packages of 2 refrigerated pie crusts for tarts, 1 package for pies

2 eggs, lightly beaten with a little water

First find a big bowl you can live without for a day or two. Then cut up the apples, zest the citrus, chop the cherries and mix them up with the raisins, currants, almonds, sugar, spices and liquors. Mix thoroughly to get an even coating. Melt the butter and mix it in completely. Cover the bowl with clear plastic wrap and set in a quiet place for 12- 48 hours. Longer would be better. The fridge is too cold, and anywhere near the stove or a heating vent will be too warm. Check the mince a few times by stirring it up and checking how much liquid is in the bowl. If it looks dry, add more brandy just to moisten. Make sure the raisins and currants are plumping up from absorbing the juices in the bowl.

Once you're ready to make your tarts or pies, preheat your oven to 350 degrees and unroll the pie crusts. Use a biscuit cutter to cut out 24 3-inch circles to fit your muffin pans. Each pie gets a top and a bottom crust. If you are making a large one, just follow the instructions for a two crust pie on the package. Lightly grease your muffin pans and place a circle of dough in each one and press it gently into the pan, and form a little edge along the top. Fill each one with a nice heaping mound of mincemeat. Brush the egg mixture on the outside edges of each bottom crust. Then, put a top crust on each one, pinching the edges tightly to seal each pie. Cut a little X on the top of each one, and brush each tart of each pie with the remaining egg mixture for a shiny, browned crust, and bake for 30 - 40 minutes or until the tops are browned and crisp. Let the tarts cool before popping them out of the pans and serve with whipped cream, ice cream or custard sauce. (see the Rhubarb Crumble recipe for custard sauce.)

Nut Brittle

Master Wizards

Makes 2 pounds

Candy making is nearly a lost art, as it is tricky and requires some patience and can be a little dangerous if you have little wizards about the house. Get them to go outside and hunt for pixies until you are finished. Also, be very careful with the hot sugar mixture, since it will stick to you as it burns, like the ancient Greek Fire of legend. You will need to have a high-heat or candy thermometer for this recipe and a plant mister type spray bottle or a very clean pastry brush. You should also ensure that the pot you use is extremely clean, as one speck of something can crystallize the sugar and ruin the recipe.

4 cups sugar

½ cup water

1/8 tsp cream of tartar

2 Tbsp unsalted butter, cut into small pieces

2 cups nuts

Nonstick pan spray, as needed

Before you start the recipe, coat a cookie sheet with sides with nonstick spray and chill it in the refrigerator. In a deep, heavy bottomed saucepan, heat the sugar, water and cream of tartar. Clip the thermometer to the side of the pot, with the bulb immersed in the sugar solution. Let the mixture reach a gentle boil and use a plant mister or pastry brush to wet the sides of the pot and thermometer frequently, to dissolve any sugar crystals that may be trying to form. Cook the sugar until it reaches the light caramel stage, which is measured at 320 degrees. Using a wooden spoon or high heat resistant rubber spatula that has also been coated with the nonstick spray, quickly stir in the butter and nuts, making sure they get completely incorporated. Then, pour the caramel and nuts into the pan and quickly spread it out evenly with a metal spatula coated with nonstick spray. Let cool for 30 minutes, and then tap the brittle gently with a hammer to break it into large pieces. Store in an airtight container away from heat or moisture.

Homemade Strawberry Ice Cream

Initiate Wizards

Makes approximately 1 quart

There is story about a mean old witch who lived alone in a magic frozen castle made of ice cream. One year there was a famine in the nearby village, but she wouldn't let the starving people eat any of her ice cream palace. The story goes on to include a valiant knight, perhaps his name was Sir Waffle Cone, who comes to save the day, defeats the witch, the villagers eat the ice cream, and they all live happily ever after. You should be able to find an inexpensive, self-churning electric ice cream machine at discount department store. Just grab a big bag of ice and some rock salt on your way home and you're in business! Make sure you have some plastic containers with lids to freeze the ice cream in when it finishes churning.

1 ¾ cups half & half

1 ½ cups heavy cream

7 egg yolks

1 cup sugar

¼ tsp vanilla extract

Pinch salt

1 cup strawberries, washed, hulled and sliced.

In a heavy pan, bring the half & half and cream to a boil. Whisk the egg yolks with the sugar and salt until the sugar is dissolved and the yolks are a pale lemon color.

Slowly add the hot liquid to the eggs, careful not to add too much too quickly, as you might end up with scrambled eggs. Return everything to the pot and cook until it starts to thicken, stirring constantly with a high heat resistant spatula. When it has thickened considerably and coats the spatula , remove the custard from the heat. Strain the custard through a fine mesh sieve and chill in a metal or glass bowl until cold. Load the ice cream machine with salt and ice as directed by the manufacturer and churn as directed. When the ice cream looks fairly thick and almost finished, add the strawberries and let them mix in for the last few minutes of churning. Scrape all the ice cream out with a rubber spatula and pack it into containers, then freeze.

Flavor Variations:

You can substitute just about any other fruit or candy bits for the strawberries. Just add them in the same manner, at the end of the churning time.

Chocolate ice cream: Melt 4 ounces of chocolate in the hot cream and half & half before whisking into the eggs.

Rum Raisin ice cream: Heat up ¼ cup dark rum and soak ½ cup seedless raisins in it until they are plump and most of the rum is absorbed. Add to ice cream as you would with other fruit, including any unabsorbed rum left from the raisins.

Herbal or flavor infused ice creams: Add pieces of herbs to the half & half and cream as you heat it and let steep 10 minutes before whisking in the eggs. Cook the custard as usual and strain the custard through a sieve to remove the herbs before you cool the mixture. Try lavender buds, sage, mint, basil, cardamom, cinnamon sticks, split vanilla beans, whole coffee beans, or whatever you want.

Ripples: To make a ripple of hot fudge, butterscotch, caramel or some other dessert sauce, you must wait until the ice cream is being packed into containers. Drizzle some of the cold sauce onto the ice cream and drag a spoon through in a swirly zigzag pattern a few times, then freeze.

Pumpkin Punch

Novice Wizards

Makes 2 quarts

Everyone likes pumpkins, Halloween and witchy things! Make up a big batch of this for your next spooky themed party and float little plastic toy spiders and stuff in it. You could even drop some dry ice in there to turn your punchbowl into a smoking cauldron.

2qt bottle of white grape or apple juice, chilled

1 can of solid pack pumpkin

Any juice you may have from making pumpkin pasties

4 inch piece of cheesecloth

Rubber bands

Open the bottle of juice and pour yourself a small glass. You need space in the bottle for the pumpkin, so just drink the juice while you make the rest of the recipe. Using a spoon, feed the pumpkin to the bottle and add any pumpkin juice you may have. Shake like mad and place in the refrigerator. Let it rest one hour. Take the cheesecloth and fold it into a small square and fit it over the mouth of the juice bottle. Use the rubber band to hold it tightly in place. The pulpy bits of the pumpkin will stay inside the bottle as you pour it into pitchers or a punchbowl.

Caramel Apples

Novice Wizards/ Classroom recipe

Makes 10 apples

Always a crowd pleaser, caramel apples can be as simple or as grand as you want. Keep in mind the size of the apples you are using and the amount of toppings you are adding. A gigantic apple looks great but who has a mouth that wide? This recipe is designed for use in classrooms or parties where everybody can make their own apple. If you need to make these ahead of time, you should refrigerate the finished apples until you are ready to eat. You'll want some disposable pans for the toppings and paper plates to catch drips and toppings.

10 medium red apples, stems removed

2 pounds store bought caramels

¼ cup water

Thick 5 inch wooden skewers

Chopped nuts

Mini chocolate chips

Colored sprinkles/ jimmies

Toasted coconut

Candy Bits

Have everyone help unwrap the caramels and put them in a metal or glass bowl. Get all your toppings, put them in the pans and line them up on a long table. Have the apples in a basket or bowl at one end, next to the skewers. Fill a pot of water, put it on the stove and heat it to almost boiling. Take ¼ cup of the hot water and add it to the caramels. Place the bowl on top of the pot of hot water and stir the caramels and hot water until melted and totally smooth. Take the bowl off the pot but leave the pot on the stove in case you need to re-melt the caramel. Wrap the bowl in a dry towel and place it next to the apples. Each person chooses their apple, sticks the skewer in the stem end and then dips the apple into the caramel, scraping the drips off on the side of the bowl. Holding the apple over a paper plate, they can go and roll their apple in whatever toppings they want. Put finished apples on paper plates to let cool and harden a few minutes before eating. Dipped apples will last 3 days, covered in the refrigerator as long as they haven't been bitten into!

Chocolate Wands

Novice Wizards/Classroom recipe

Fun to make with a crowd, these wands won't do much more than make a mess if you insist on trying to cast a spells with them, so just eat it instead. The idea is to have everything ready and let everyone make their own wand. The amounts given make enough wands for about 20 people. Increase or decrease the amounts to suit your needs. These are perfect for younger wizards and their professors to make in school as a group project.

Again, you'll want some disposable pans for the toppings and paper plates to catch drips and toppings.

1 or 2 bags of pretzel rods

2 pounds milk chocolate, broken into small pieces

2 pounds white chocolate, broken into small pieces

3 or 4 kinds of candy bars about 6 each

1 bag mini peanut butter chips

1 bag mini chocolate chips

Colored sprinkles/jimmies

Colored coarse decorating sugar

Toasted shredded coconut

Chopped mixed nuts

First, freeze the candy bars for a few hours, then unwrap them, and place each kind inside a thick plastic freezer bag. Smash the candy into little bits with a meat mallet or hammer. Pour each bag of candy bar bits into its own pan. Pour all the other decorations into their own pans and line them up on a long table. On the stovetop, heat two pots of water to a steady simmer, not quite a boil. Put the white chocolate in a metal or glass bowl and the milk chocolate in another. Place each bowl on top of each pot so the hot water melts the chocolate without burning. Stir each bowl of chocolate often to see how melted it is and to scrape any chocolate on the sides of the bowl back into the center. Once the chocolate is melted and smooth, remove each bowl from the heat and dry off the bottoms of the bowls. Wrap them in thick kitchen towels to keep warm. Set both bowls at one end of the table. Keep at least one pot of simmering water on the stove while you decorate the wands. Eventually the chocolate will start to harden, just put the bowl back onto the pot on the stove and reheat until melted, smooth and shiny again.

Let everyone grab a pretzel rod and line up at the chocolate end of the table. Dip ¾ of each pretzel into either chocolate and let drip a moment or two. Holding paper plates under their wand to catch drips, everybody can now move down the line and roll their wand in whatever they want, pressing down to stick the little bits to the chocolate on the wand. Those who want to "double dip" for two color wands have to wait at least 10 minutes between dips to let the first application of chocolate harden completely or it will slip off the wand into the other bowl. Have fun waving the wands around and comparing decorating techniques, then eat!

Treacle Toffee

Master Wizards

Makes 16 pieces

This candy was once used to glue naughty children's mouths shut by a very sweet witch who just wasn't evil enough to curse or eat the children. She would feed them a piece of this when they started calling her names and their mouths would stay closed long enough for her to run away. Be careful with boiling sugar solutions, they are much hotter than boiling water and a lot stickier. Have hot pads and cold running water available at all times. You will need a candy thermometer and an 8x8 inch glass baking dish for this recipe. Wrapping the pieces of toffee in waxed paper makes it look as if it just came from a candy store.

1 pound brown sugar

4 ounces treacle

2 ounces butter

1 cup milk

4 inch waxed paper squares

Butcher's twine

Nonstick cooking spray

First, spray the baking dish with the nonstick spray and chill in the refrigerator.

In a deep, heavy pot, heat the milk with the treacle and sugar over medium to low heat. Clip the candy thermometer to the side of the pot so the bulb is immersed. Cook until the thermometer reads 270 degrees, just below "soft crack" stage. This could take longer than you think. It's easy for liquids to reach the boiling point at 212 degrees, but after that it's a long slow crawl up the thermometer. Remove from the heat and add the butter bit by bit. Stir it in with a high heat resistant spatula that has been sprayed with the nonstick cooking spray. Pour the syrup evenly into the prepared pan. Return the pan to the fridge to cool the candy for about an hour. Unmold the toffee by turning it out onto a cutting board. Cut into one inch squares, using a ruler if you need to. Wrap each piece individually with waxed paper and tie it closed with the butcher's twine.

Trifle

Master Wizards (unless you omit the alcohol for **Novice Wizards**)

Serves 8 - 10

Packed with fruit, creamy custard and liquor soaked cake, this summery dessert will have you on your way to the land of the fairies in no time. If very young wizards are going to be eating this, it may be best to omit the liquors. This decadent dessert looks its best when served in a deep, footed glass bowl so everyone can see the layers.

1 store bought pound cake, cut into 1 inch slices

½ cup seedless raspberry jam, jelly or preserves

1 cup dark rum

¼ cup brandy

2 cups heavy whipping cream

3 Tbsp sugar

¼ tsp vanilla extract

1 package instant French Vanilla flavor pudding and milk as directed.

3 pints fresh raspberries, picked through for damaged fruit.

Start by preparing the pudding mix according to the directions for pie filling. Chill for at least ½ an hour. Then, chill your bowl and whisk for the whipped cream. Mix the brandy and rum together in a bowl. Next, spread a thin layer of the jam on each slice of the cake, and lay half the slices jam side up across the bottom of the glass dish. You may need to trim the cake slices to fit the shape of the bowl. Sprinkle half of the rum and brandy evenly over the cake slices. With an electric mixer, whip the cream with the sugar and vanilla until stiff peaks form. Chill the whipped cream while you spread half of the pudding on top of the cake. Place 1/3 of the raspberries on top of the custard. Now make another layer by spreading half of the whipped cream with a spatula to create an even layer. Place the remaining cake slices on next, and sprinkle them with the rum. Make another pudding layer, and repeat until you have filled the bowl just to the rim. Decorate it with berries, chill for an hour and serve.

Treacle Tart

Novice Wizards

Makes one 9 inch tart, 8 - 12 servings

This dessert has a habit of disappearing if left unattended. I don't know if fairies are stealing it, but it never lasts more than a night in our house. Treacle is a by-product of sugar production in the United Kingdom, like American molasses but with a malty, nuttier taste. This recipe is very easy and goes together in a matter of minutes with great results every time. Dress up the plate for company by shaking a little powdered sugar of each slice of tart and decorating each one with a raspberry and a mint leaf tucked in next to it.

One 9 inch prepared pie crust

1 ½ cups treacle

1 ½ cups fresh soft breadcrumbs. Make by putting sliced white bread in the food processor or by shredding finely with forks.

1 Tbsp lemon juice

½ tsp ground ginger

1 egg, lightly beaten

Preheat your oven to 350 degrees. Pat your pie crust into a buttered pie pan and set it in the fridge while you make the filling. In a large bowl, combine all the other ingredients and stir until well mixed. Pour the mixture into the pie shell, and tap the sides of the pan to pop any air bubbles. Bake the tart in the middle of the oven for 40 to 50 minutes or until the filling is firm and browned. Let it cool for at least an hour, as it needs to firm up after baking.

Pumpkin Pie Pockets

Novice Wizards

Makes 12

An old favorite gone portable, these are really easy to make and also fit pretty well in a lunchbox. Draining the excess liquid out of the pumpkin keeps the filling thick and you can use the liquid you collect for making pumpkin juice. Decorating with colored sugar makes a nice sparkly crust and adds a little sweetness. Serve these at Halloween parties or a spooky birthday party, or whenever you want pumpkin pie!

1 package of 2 refrigerated prepared pie crusts

1 can solid pack pumpkin, drained

2 tsp pumpkin pie spice

½ cup sugar

¼ cup brown sugar

4 oz block cream cheese

2 eggs

Water, as needed

Yellow or orange coarse decorating sugar

First, drain the pumpkin by emptying the can into a mesh sieve lined with a coffee filter. Place the sieve over a bowl to collect to juice and let it drain for an hour. Gently press the pumpkin with the back of a spoon the get more juice out.

Using an electric mixer beat the cream cheese and both sugars on high speed until smooth and fluffy. Then, add one egg and mix until the egg is totally incorporated. Add the spices, salt, and drained pumpkin, and beat on high speed until the whole mixture is smooth and light. Chill this mixture while you prepare the crusts.

Heat your oven to 375 degrees. Gently unroll both pie crusts on a clean, flat surface. Cut twelve 3 inch circles out of the dough. Flatten out each circle with a rolling pin to make it

A little bigger and thinner, but be sure to keep it in a circular shape. To make the pockets lightly brush the edges of each dough circle with the other egg that has been beaten with a little bit of water. Spoon the chilled pumpkin filling to one side of each circle and fold over. Press your fingertips firmly along the edges to make an attractive looking, sealed half moon shape. Brush each one lightly with the egg mixture and sprinkle with the decorating sugar. Place each pocket on a cookie sheet and bake in the middle of the oven for 30 to 40 minutes or until fully cooked and golden brown. Let the pockets cool before serving.

Knickerbocker Glory

Novice Wizards

Serves 4

This is the most outrageous ice cream treat ever, and it hails from merry old England, home of Stonehenge. You won't need any giants or druids to help assemble this monumental dessert, though. You will want some tall parfait glasses to do this properly, but any type of glass you can add a lot of layers to will do. It's also fun to poke sparklers and those little flags on toothpicks on top and light them (just the sparklers!) just before you present this to your guests.

1 carton vanilla ice cream

1 package French Vanilla flavor instant pudding and milk as directed

1 package store bought sponge cakes

1 jar hot fudge sauce

1 jar whole fruit preserves of your choice

Can of whipped light cream, ready to use

Maraschino cherries

Chopped nuts (if you like them)

Mix the pudding, following the directions for pie filling and chill for a half an hour. Then take the ice cream out of the freezer and place it in the refrigerator to soften while you heat the hot fudge according to the directions on the jar. In each glass, start the layering with a small amount of hot fudge in each glass. Follow with some of the fruit preserves, then spoon in a layer of the pudding, tuck in a piece of sponge cake, a scoop of ice cream, the hot fudge again, and repeat each layer just once, so the ice cream is the last layer the second time, and garnish with a drizzle of hot fudge, some whipped cream, the nuts and cherry.

Powerful Potions

These are only for witches and wizards above the legal drinking age. Underage wizards who try advanced potions will end up making themselves very sick and get into trouble with their parents. It's not worth it. Wait until you are old enough, please.

Single Flagon Potions, page 62

Potions for a Crowd, page 63

Single Flagon Potions

Green Serpent

In a chilled shot glass, pour green crème de menthe to fill halfway. Carefully pour white crème de cacao on top to float. Drink in one gulp and prepare yourself for some snakelike moves on the dance floor.

Red Dragon's Fire

Pour equal amounts of Red Aftershock and Goldschlager into a chilled shot glass. Sling it back and roar like a dragon.

Hooting Owl

Add equal amounts of Chambord liqueur, Absolut Citron, and sour mix to a cocktail shaker full of ice. Shake hard for a few minutes, then strain into shot glasses. After a few of these, you might be dancing around and flapping your arms, so be careful.

Blue Surf

Fill a chilled shot glass halfway with Blue Curacao. Carefully pour coconut flavored rum to fill, floating it on top. You will feel like you just teleported to a tropical island.

Potions for a Crowd

The Kiss of Death

Makes one blender full, to be divided into 2 ounce shots. Fill the blender ¾ full of ice and add 6 ounces Rumpleminze, 6 ounces Vodka, and 6 ounces white crème de cocoa. Blend until slushy and smooth. Pour into chilled shot glasses, drink at once and hold on to your soul.

Fairy Lights

Have one bottle of champagne and one bottle of Grey Goose Vodka fully chilled beforehand. Pour champagne into flutes, filling them ¾ full. Add one ounce of vodka and ½ an ounce of Blue Curacao to each glass.

Bloody Knight

For each person, fill a tall glass with ice and add;

1 ounce Vodka

4 ounces tomato juice

½ tsp Worcestershire sauce

1 tsp lemon juice

2 to 3 drops Tabasco sauce

Stir and serve each one with a washed celery stalk with the leaves still on.

Glogg

Just the thing in wintertime. Glogg is more intense than mulled wine, with almonds and raisins as the traditional garnish. Serve this hot in coffee mugs. For a party, you can make this in an electric kettle or crock pot and let guests serve themselves.

1 bottle red wine

1 Tbsp cardamom pods

4 cinnamon sticks

1 Tbsp whole cloves

2 pieces star anise

½ cup brandy

¼ cup honey

Seedless raisins

Sliced almonds

Sugar cubes

Warm everything but the sugar cubes, raisins and almonds over low heat for one hour, careful not to let it boil. When ready to serve, place a spoonful of raisins and almonds in the bottom of each mug. Fill each mug with hot glogg and drop in a sugar cube just before serving.

Eggnog

Everyone enjoy this classic homemade eggnog. You should leave the bourbon out to serve this to those who are not old enough to imbibe or for those who just prefer it without.

6 eggs

¼ cup sugar

1 qt milk

1 vanilla bean

¼ tsp nutmeg

¼ tsp ground cinnamon

1 cup Bourbon

In a heavy bottomed saucepan, whisk together the eggs, sugar and half of the milk. Add the nutmeg and cinnamon. Split the vanilla bean lengthways with a paring knife and scrape the seeds out with the back of the knife and add them to the pot. Heat to 160 degrees, stirring constantly with a heat resistant rubber spatula, until it is thick and coats the spatula. Remove from the heat and whisk in the remaining milk and the bourbon. Chill it for 2 hours, then stir before serving.

Mulled Wine

You could make this in an electric kettle or crock pot.

1 bottle red wine

½ cup sugar

2 cinnamon sticks

1 tsp whole cloves

1 tsp whole allspice

In a deep pot, stir all the ingredients together until the sugar dissolves and place over low heat. Simmer for at least an hour. Be careful not to let it boil. Serve hot.